I'll Push, You Pull

Paul Humphrey

Illustrated by

Kat

4

5

7

8

He pulls the thread.

9

10

The rowers pull the oars.

What else pushes?

The snow plough pushes the snow off the road.

12

What else pulls?

The train pulls the trucks.

14

She pushes down on the pedals.

He pushes the wheelbarrow.

17

The man lifts the weights...

...and pushes them into the air.

19

The tractor pulls the plough.

The bulldozer pushes the earth.

I push the sledge...

...and ride!

Yippee!

Then we have to pull the sledge up the hill again.

We all push Mum's car.

24

25

We all pull in tug-of-war.

26

27

We all fall over!

29

Which things on this page push?
Which things pull?
Which things can push and pull?